The Poetry of Algernon Charles Swinburne

VOLUME VII - SONGS OF THE SPRINGTIDES & BIRTHDAY ODE

Algernon Charles Swinburne was born on April 5th, 1837, in London, into a wealthy Northumbrian family. He was educated at Eton and at Balliol College, Oxford, but did not complete a degree.

In 1860 Swinburne published two verse dramas but achieved his first literary success in 1865 with Atalanta in Calydon, written in the form of classical Greek tragedy. The following year "Poems and Ballads" brought him instant notoriety. He was now identified with "indecent" themes and the precept of art for art's sake.

Although he produced much after this success in general his popularity and critical reputation declined. The most important qualities of Swinburne's work are an intense lyricism, his intricately extended and evocative imagery, metrical virtuosity, rich use of assonance and alliteration, and bold, complex rhythms.

Swinburne's physical appearance was small, frail, and plagued by several other oddities of physique and temperament. Throughout the 1860s and 1870s he drank excessively and was prone to accidents that often left him bruised, bloody, or unconscious. Until his forties he suffered intermittent physical collapses that necessitated removal to his parents' home while he recovered.

Throughout his career Swinburne also published literary criticism of great worth. His deep knowledge of world literatures contributed to a critical style rich in quotation, allusion, and comparison. He is particularly noted for discerning studies of Elizabethan dramatists and of many English and French poets and novelists. As well he was a noted essayist and wrote two novels.

In 1879, Swinburne's friend and literary agent, Theodore Watts-Dunton, intervened during a time when Swinburne was dangerously ill. Watts-Dunton isolated Swinburne at a suburban home in Putney and gradually weaned him from alcohol, former companions and many other habits as well.

Much of his poetry in this period may be inferior but some individual poems are exceptional; "By the North Sea," "Evening on the Broads," "A Nympholept," "The Lake of Gaube," and "Neap-Tide."

Swinburne lived another thirty years with Watts-Dunton. He denied Swinburne's friends access to him, controlled the poet's money, and restricted his activities. It is often quoted that 'he saved the man but killed the poet'.

Swinburne died on April 10th, 1909 at the age of seventy-two.

Index of Contents

SONGS OF THE SPRINGTIDES

DEDICATION TO EDWARD JOHN TRELAWNY

A sea-mew on a sea-king's wrist alighting,
As the north sea-wind caught and strained and curled
The raven-figured flag that led men fighting
From field to green field of the water-world,
Might find such brief high favour at his hand
For wings imbrued with brine, with foam impearled,
As these my songs require at yours on land,
That durst not save for love's free sake require,
Being lightly born between the foam and sand,
But reared by hope and memory and desire
Of lives that were and life that is to be,
Even such as filled his heavenlier song with fire
Whose very voice, that sang to set man free,
Was in your ears as ever in ours his lyre,
Once, ere the flame received him from the sea.

THALASSIUS

Upon the flowery forefront of the year,
One wandering by the grey-green April sea
Found on a reach of shingle and shallower sand
Inlaid with starrier glimmering jewellery
Left for the sun's love and the light wind's cheer
Along the foam-flowered strand
Breeze-brightened, something nearer sea than land
Though the last shoreward blossom-fringe was near,
A babe asleep with flower-soft face that gleamed
To sun and seaward as it laughed and dreamed,
Too sure of either love for either's fear,
Albeit so birdlike slight and light, it seemed
Nor man nor mortal child of man, but fair
As even its twin-born tenderer spray-flowers were,
That the wind scatters like an Oread's hair.

For when July strewed fire on earth and sea
The last time ere that year,
Out of the flame of morn Cymothoe
Beheld one brighter than the sunbright sphere
Move toward her from its fieriest heart, whence trod
The live sun's very God,
Across the foam-bright water-ways that are
As heavenlier heavens with star for answering star,
And on her eyes and hair and maiden mouth
Felt a kiss falling fierier than the South
And heard above afar
A noise of songs and wind-enamoured wings
And lutes and lyres of milder and mightier strings,
And round the resonant radiance of his car
Where depth is one with height,
Light heard as music, music seen as light.
And with that second moondawn of the spring's
That fosters the first rose,
A sun-child whiter than the sunlit snows
Was born out of the world of sunless things
That round the round earth flows and ebbs and flows.

But he that found the sea-flower by the sea
And took to foster like a graft of earth
Was born of man's most highest and heavenliest birth,
Free-born as winds and stars and waves are free;
A warrior grey with glories more than years,
Though more of years than change the quick to dead
Had rained their light and darkness on his head;
A singer that in time's and memory's ears
Should leave such words to sing as all his peers
Might praise with hallowing heat of rapturous tears
Till all the days of human flight were fled.
And at his knees his fosterling was fed
Not with man's wine and bread
Nor mortal mother-milk of hopes and fears,
But food of deep memorial days long sped;
For bread with wisdom and with song for wine
Clear as the full calm's emerald hyaline.
And from his grave glad lips the boy would gather
Fine honey of song-notes goldener than gold,
More sweet than bees make of the breathing heather,
That he, as glad and bold,
Might drink as they, and keep his spirit from cold.
And the boy loved his laurel-laden hair
As his own father's risen on the eastern air,
And that less white brow-binding bayleaf bloom
More than all flowers his father's eyes relume;

And those high songs he heard,
More than all notes of any landward bird,
More than all sounds less free
Than the wind's quiring to the choral sea.

High things the high song taught him; how the breath
Too frail for life may be more strong than death;
And this poor flash of sense in life, that gleams
As a ghost's glory in dreams,
More stabile than the world's own heart's root seems,
By that strong faith of lordliest love which gives
To death's own sightless-seeming eyes a light
Clearer, to death's bare bones a verier might,
Than shines or strikes from any man that lives.
How he that loves life overmuch shall die
The dog's death, utterly:
And he that much less loves it than he hates
All wrongdoing that is done
Anywhere always underneath the sun
Shall live a mightier life than time's or fate's.
One fairer thing he shewed him, and in might
More strong than day and night
Whose strengths build up time's towering period:
Yea, one thing stronger and more high than God,
Which if man had not, then should God not be:
And that was Liberty.
And gladly should man die to gain, he said,
Freedom; and gladlier, having lost, lie dead.
For man's earth was not, nor the sweet sea-waves
His, nor his own land, nor its very graves,
Except they bred not, bore not, hid not slaves:
But all of all that is,
Were one man free in body and soul, were his.

And the song softened, even as heaven by night
Softens, from sunnier down to starrier light,
And with its moonbright breath
Blessed life for death's sake, and for life's sake death.
Till as the moon's own beam and breath confuse
In one clear hueless haze of glimmering hues
The sea's line and the land's line and the sky's,
And light for love of darkness almost dies,
As darkness only lives for light's dear love,
Whose hands the web of night is woven of,
So in that heaven of wondrous words were life
And death brought out of strife;
Yea, by that strong spell of serene increase
Brought out of strife to peace.

And the song lightened, as the wind at morn
Flashes, and even with lightning of the wind
Night's thick-spun web is thinned
And all its weft unwoven and overworn
Shrinks, as might love from scorn.
And as when wind and light on water and land
Leap as twin gods from heavenward hand in hand,
And with the sound and splendour of their leap
Strike darkness dead, and daunt the spirit of sleep,
And burn it up with fire;
So with the light that lightened from the lyre
Was all the bright heat in the child's heart stirred
And blown with blasts of music into flame
Till even his sense became
Fire, as the sense that fires the singing bird
Whose song calls night by name.
And in the soul within the sense began
The manlike passion of a godlike man,
And in the sense within the soul again
Thoughts that make men of gods and gods of men.

For love the high song taught him: love that turns
God's heart toward man as man's to Godward; love
That life and death and life are fashioned of,
From the first breath that burns
Half kindled on the flowerlike yeanling's lip,
So light and faint that life seems like to slip,
To that yet weaklier drawn
When sunset dies of night's devouring dawn.
But the man dying not wholly as all men dies
If aught be left of his in live men's eyes
Out of the dawnless dark of death to rise;
If aught of deed or word
Be seen for all time or of all time heard.
Love, that though body and soul were overthrown
Should live for love's sake of itself alone,
Though spirit and flesh were one thing doomed and dead,
Not wholly annihilated.
Seeing even the hoariest ash-flake that the pyre
Drops, and forgets the thing was once afire
And gave its heart to feed the pile's full flame
Till its own heart its own heat overcame,
Outlives its own life, though by scarce a span,
As such men dying outlive themselves in man,
Outlive themselves for ever; if the heat
Outburn the heart that kindled it, the sweet
Outlast the flower whose soul it was, and flit

Forth of the body of it
Into some new shape of a strange perfume
More potent than its light live spirit of bloom,
How shall not something of that soul relive,
That only soul that had such gifts to give
As lighten something even of all men's doom
Even from the labouring womb
Even to the seal set on the unopening tomb?
And these the loving light of song and love
Shall wrap and lap round and impend above,
Imperishable; and all springs born illume
Their sleep with brighter thoughts than wake the dove
To music, when the hillside winds resume
The marriage-song of heather-flower and broom
And all the joy thereof.

And hate the song too taught him: hate of all
That brings or holds in thrall
Of spirit or flesh, free-born ere God began,
The holy body and sacred soul of man.
And wheresoever a curse was or a chain,
A throne for torment or a crown for bane
Rose, moulded out of poor men's molten pain,
There, said he, should man's heaviest hate be set
Inexorably, to faint not or forget
Till the last warmth bled forth of the last vein
In flesh that none should call a king's again,
Seeing wolves and dogs and birds that plague-strike air
Leave the last bone of all the carrion bare.

And hope the high song taught him: hope whose eyes
Can sound the seas unsoundable, the skies
Inaccessible of eyesight; that can see
What earth beholds not, hear what wind and sea
Hear not, and speak what all these crying in one
Can speak not to the sun.
For in her sovereign eyelight all things are
Clear as the closest seen and kindlier star
That marries morn and even and winter and spring
With one love's golden ring.
For she can see the days of man, the birth
Of good and death of evil things on earth
Inevitable and infinite, and sure
As present pain is, or herself is pure.
Yea, she can hear and see, beyond all things
That lighten from before Time's thunderous wings
Through the awful circle of wheel-winged periods,
The tempest of the twilight of all Gods:

And higher than all the circling course they ran
The sundawn of the spirit that was man.

And fear the song too taught him; fear to be
Worthless the dear love of the wind and sea
That bred him fearless, like a sea-mew reared
In rocks of man's foot feared,
Where nought of wingless life may sing or shine.
Fear to wax worthless of that heaven he had
When all the life in all his limbs was glad
And all the drops in all his veins were wine
And all the pulses music; when his heart,
Singing, bade heaven and wind and sea bear part
In one live song's reiterance, and they bore:
Fear to go crownless of the flower he wore
When the winds loved him and the waters knew,
The blithest life that clove their blithe life through
With living limbs exultant, or held strife
More amorous than all dalliance aye anew
With the bright breath and strength of their large life,
With all strong wrath of all sheer winds that blew,
All glories of all storms of the air that fell
Prone, ineluctable,
With roar from heaven of revel, and with hue
As of a heaven turned hell.
For when the red blast of their breath had made
All heaven aflush with light more dire than shade,
He felt it in his blood and eyes and hair
Burn as if all the fires of the earth and air
Had laid strong hold upon his flesh, and stung
The soul behind it as with serpent's tongue,
Forked like the loveliest lightnings: nor could bear
But hardly, half distraught with strong delight,
The joy that like a garment wrapped him round
And lapped him over and under
With raiment of great light
And rapture of great sound
At every loud leap earthward of the thunder
From heaven's most furthest bound:
So seemed all heaven in hearing and in sight,
Alive and mad with glory and angry joy,
That something of its marvellous mirth and might
Moved even to madness, fledged as even for flight,
The blood and spirit of one but mortal boy.

So, clothed with love and fear that love makes great,
And armed with hope and hate,
He set first foot upon the spring-flowered ways

That all feet pass and praise.
And one dim dawn between the winter and spring,
In the sharp harsh wind harrying heaven and earth
To put back April that had borne his birth
From sunward on her sunniest shower-struck wing,
With tears and laughter for the dew-dropt thing,
Slight as indeed a dew-drop, by the sea
One met him lovelier than all men may be,
God-featured, with god's eyes; and in their might
Somewhat that drew men's own to mar their sight,
Even of all eyes drawn toward him: and his mouth
Was as the very rose of all men's youth,
One rose of all the rose-beds in the world:
But round his brows the curls were snakes that curled,
And like his tongue a serpent's; and his voice
Speaks death, and bids rejoice.
Yet then he spake no word, seeming as dumb,
A dumb thing mild and hurtless; nor at first
From his bowed eyes seemed any light to come,
Nor his meek lips for blood or tears to thirst:
But as one blind and mute in mild sweet wise
Pleading for pity of piteous lips and eyes,
He strayed with faint bare lily-lovely feet
Helpless, and flowerlike sweet:
Nor might man see, not having word hereof,
That this of all gods was the great god Love.

And seeing him lovely and like a little child
That wellnigh wept for wonder that it smiled
And was so feeble and fearful, with soft speech
The youth bespake him softly; but there fell
From the sweet lips no sweet word audible
That ear or thought might reach:
No sound to make the dim cold silence glad,
No breath to thaw the hard harsh air with heat;
Only the saddest smile of all things sweet,
Only the sweetest smile of all things sad.

And so they went together one green way
Till April dying made free the world for May;
And on his guide suddenly Love's face turned,
And in his blind eyes burned
Hard light and heat of laughter; and like flame
That opens in a mountain's ravening mouth
To blear and sear the sunlight from the south,
His mute mouth opened, and his first word came:
'Knowest thou me now by name?'
And all his stature waxed immeasurable,

As of one shadowing heaven and lightening hell;
And statelier stood he than a tower that stands
And darkens with its darkness far-off sands
Whereon the sky leans red;
And with a voice that stilled the winds he said:
'I am he that was thy lord before thy birth,
I am he that is thy lord till thou turn earth:
I make the night more dark, and all the morrow
Dark as the night whose darkness was my breath:
O fool, my name is sorrow;
Thou fool, my name is death.'

And he that heard spake not, and looked right on
Again, and Love was gone.

Through many a night toward many a wearier day
His spirit bore his body down its way.
Through many a day toward many a wearier night
His soul sustained his sorrows in her sight.
And earth was bitter, and heaven, and even the sea
Sorrowful even as he.
And the wind helped not, and the sun was dumb;
And with too long strong stress of grief to be
His heart grew sere and numb.

And one bright eve ere summer in autumn sank
At stardawn standing on a grey sea-bank
He felt the wind fitfully shift and heave
As toward a stormier eve;
And all the wan wide sea shuddered; and earth
Shook underfoot as toward some timeless birth,
Intolerable and inevitable; and all
Heaven, darkling, trembled like a stricken thrall.
And far out of the quivering east, and far
From past the moonrise and its guiding star,
Began a noise of tempest and a light
That was not of the lightning; and a sound
Rang with it round and round
That was not of the thunder; and a flight
As of blown clouds by night,
That was not of them; and with songs and cries
That sang and shrieked their soul out at the skies
A shapeless earthly storm of shapes began
From all ways round to move in on the man,
Clamorous against him silent; and their feet
Were as the wind's are fleet,
And their shrill songs were as wild birds' are sweet.

And as when all the world of earth was wronged
And all the host of all men driven afoam
By the red hand of Rome,
Round some fierce amphitheatre overthronged
With fair clear faces full of bloodier lust
Than swells and stings the tiger when his mood
Is fieriest after blood
And drunk with trampling of the murderous must
That soaks and stains the tortuous close-coiled wood
Made monstrous with its myriad-mustering brood,
Face by fair face panted and gleamed and pressed,
And breast by passionate breast
Heaved hot with ravenous rapture, as they quaffed
The red ripe full fume of the deep live draught,
The sharp quick reek of keen fresh bloodshed, blown
Through the dense deep drift up to the emperor's throne
From the under steaming sands
With clamour of all-applausive throats and hands,
Mingling in mirthful time
With shrill blithe mockeries of the lithe-limbed mime:
So from somewhence far forth of the unbeholden,
Dreadfully driven from over and after and under,
Fierce, blown through fifes of brazen blast and golden,
With sound of chiming waves that drown the thunder
Or thunder that strikes dumb the sea's own chimes,
Began the bellowing of the bull-voiced mimes,
Terrible; firs bowed down as briars or palms
Even at the breathless blast as of a breeze
Fulfilled with clamour and clangour and storms of psalms;
Red hands rent up the roots of old-world trees,
Thick flames of torches tossed as tumbling seas
Made mad the moonless and infuriate air
That, ravening, revelled in the riotous hair
And raiment of the furred Bassarides.

So came all those in on him; and his heart,
As out of sleep suddenly struck astart,
Danced, and his flesh took fire of theirs, and grief
Was as a last year's leaf
Blown dead far down the wind's way; and he set
His pale mouth to the brightest mouth it met
That laughed for love against his lips, and bade
Follow; and in following all his blood grew glad
And as again a sea-bird's; for the wind
Took him to bathe him deep round breast and brow
Not as it takes a dead leaf drained and thinned,
But as the brightest bay-flower blown on bough,
Set springing toward it singing: and they rode

By many a vine-leafed, many a rose-hung road,
Exalt with exultation; many a night
Set all its stars upon them as for spies
On many a moon-bewildering mountain-height
Where he rode only by the fierier light
Of his dread lady's hot sweet hungering eyes.
For the moon wandered witless of her way,
Spell-stricken by strong magic in such wise
As wizards use to set the stars astray.
And in his ears the music that makes mad
Beat always; and what way the music bade,
That alway rode he; nor was any sleep
His, nor from height nor deep.
But heaven was as red iron, slumberless,
And had no heart to bless;
And earth lay sere and darkling as distraught,
And help in her was nought.

Then many a midnight, many a morn and even,
His mother, passing forth of her fair heaven,
With goodlier gifts than all save gods can give
From earth or from the heaven where sea-things live,
With shine of sea-flowers through the bay-leaf braid
Woven for a crown her foam-white hands had made
To crown him with land's laurel and sea-dew,
Sought the sea-bird that was her boy: but he
Sat panther-throned beside Erigone,
Riding the red ways of the revel through
Midmost of pale-mouthed passion's crownless crew.
Till on some winter's dawn of some dim year
He let the vine-bit on the panther's lip
Slide, and the green rein slip,
And set his eyes to seaward, nor gave ear
If sound from landward hailed him, dire or dear;
And passing forth of all those fair fierce ranks
Back to the grey sea-banks,
Against a sea-rock lying, aslant the steep,
Fell after many sleepless dreams on sleep.

And in his sleep the dun green light was shed
Heavily round his head
That through the veil of sea falls fathom-deep,
Blurred like a lamp's that when the night drops dead
Dies; and his eyes gat grace of sleep to see
The deep divine dark dayshine of the sea,
Dense water-walls and clear dusk water-ways,
Broad-based, or branching as a sea-flower sprays
That side or this dividing; and anew

The glory of all her glories that he knew.
And in sharp rapture of recovering tears
He woke on fire with yearnings of old years,
Pure as one purged of pain that passion bore,
Ill child of bitter mother; for his own
Looked laughing toward him from her midsea throne,
Up toward him there ashore.

Thence in his heart the great same joy began,
Of child that made him man:
And turned again from all hearts else on quest,
He communed with his own heart, and had rest.
And like sea-winds upon loud waters ran
His days and dreams together, till the joy
Burned in him of the boy.
Till the earth's great comfort and the sweet sea's breath
Breathed and blew life in where was heartless death,
Death spirit-stricken of soul-sick days, where strife
Of thought and flesh made mock of death and life.
And grace returned upon him of his birth
Where heaven was mixed with heavenlike sea and earth;
And song shot forth strong wings that took the sun
From inward, fledged with might of sorrow and mirth
And father's fire made mortal in his son.
Nor was not spirit of strength in blast and breeze
To exalt again the sun's child and the sea's;
For as wild mares in Thessaly grow great
With child of ravishing winds, that violate
Their leaping length of limb with manes like fire
And eyes outburning heaven's
With fires more violent than the lightning levin's
And breath drained out and desperate of desire,
Even so the spirit in him, when winds grew strong,
Grew great with child of song.
Nor less than when his veins first leapt for joy
To draw delight in such as burns a boy,
Now too the soul of all his senses felt
The passionate pride of deep sea-pulses dealt
Through nerve and jubilant vein
As from the love and largess of old time,
And with his heart again
The tidal throb of all the tides keep rhyme
And charm him from his own soul's separate sense
With infinite and invasive influence
That made strength sweet in him and sweetness strong,
Being now no more a singer, but a song.

Till one clear day when brighter sea-wind blew

And louder sea-shine lightened, for the waves
Were full of godhead and the light that saves,
His father's, and their spirit had pierced him through,
He felt strange breath and light all round him shed
That bowed him down with rapture; and he knew
His father's hand, hallowing his humbled head,
And the old great voice of the old good time, that said:

"Child of my sunlight and the sea, from birth
A fosterling and fugitive on earth;
Sleepless of soul as wind or wave or fire,
A manchild with an ungrown God's desire;
Because thou hast loved nought mortal more than me,
Thy father, and thy mother-hearted sea;
Because thou hast set thine heart to sing, and sold
Life and life's love for song, God's living gold;
Because thou hast given thy flower and fire of youth
To feed men's hearts with visions, truer than truth;
Because thou hast kept in those world-wandering eyes
The light that makes me music of the skies;
Because thou hast heard with world-unwearied ears
The music that puts light into the spheres;
Have therefore in thine heart and in thy mouth
The sound of song that mingles north and south,
The song of all the winds that sing of me,
And in thy soul the sense of all the sea."

ON THE CLIFFS

Between the moondawn and the sundown here
The twilight hangs half starless; half the sea
Still quivers as for love or pain or fear
Or pleasure mightier than these all may be
A man's live heart might beat
Wherein a God's with mortal blood should meet
And fill its pulse too full to bear the strain
With fear or love or pleasure's twin-born, pain.
Fiercely the gaunt woods to the grim soil cling
That bears for all fair fruits
Wan wild sparse flowers of windy and wintry spring
Between the tortive serpent-shapen roots
Wherethrough their dim growth hardly strikes and shoots
And shews one gracious thing
Hardly, to speak for summer one sweet word
Of summer's self scarce heard.
But higher the steep green sterile fields, thick-set

With flowerless hawthorn even to the upward verge
Whence the woods gathering watch new cliffs emerge
Higher than their highest of crowns that sea-winds fret,
Hold fast, for all that night or wind can say,
Some pale pure colour yet,
Too dim for green and luminous for grey.
Between the climbing inland cliffs above
And these beneath that breast and break the bay,
A barren peace too soft for hate or love
Broods on an hour too dim for night or day.

O wind, O wingless wind that walk'st the sea,
Weak wind, wing-broken, wearier wind than we,
Who are yet not spirit-broken, maimed like thee,
Who wail not in our inward night as thou
In the outer darkness now,
What word has the old sea given thee for mine ear
From thy faint lips to hear?
For some word would she send me, knowing not how.

Nay, what far other word
Than ever of her was spoken, or of me
Or all my winged white kinsfolk of the sea
Between fresh wave and wave was ever heard,
Cleaves the clear dark enwinding tree with tree
Too close for stars to separate and to see
Enmeshed in multitudinous unity?
What voice of what strong God hath stormed and stirred
The fortressed rock of silence, rent apart
Even to the core Night's all-maternal heart?
What voice of God grown heavenlier in a bird,
Made keener of edge to smite
Than lightning--yea, thou knowest, O mother Night,
Keen as that cry from thy strange children sent
Wherewith the Athenian judgment-shrine was rent,
For wrath that all their wrath was vainly spent,
Their wrath for wrong made right
By justice in her own divine despite
That bade pass forth unblamed
The sinless matricide and unashamed?
Yea, what new cry is this, what note more bright
Than their song's wing of words was dark of flight,
What word is this thou hast heard,
Thine and not thine or theirs, O Night, what word
More keen than lightning and more sweet than light?
As all men's hearts grew godlike in one bird
And all those hearts cried on thee, crying with might,
Hear us, O mother Night.

Dumb is the mouth of darkness as of death:
Light, sound and life are one
In the eyes and lips of dawn that draw the sun
To hear what first child's word with glimmering breath
Their weak wan weanling child the twilight saith;
But night makes answer none.

God, if thou be God,--bird, if bird thou be,--
Do thou then answer me.
For but one word, what wind soever blow,
Is blown up usward ever from the sea.
In fruitless years of youth dead long ago
And deep beneath their own dead leaves and snow
Buried, I heard with bitter heart and sere
The same sea's word unchangeable, nor knew
But that mine own life-days were changeless too
And sharp and salt with unshed tear on tear
And cold and fierce and barren; and my soul,
Sickening, swam weakly with bated breath
In a deep sea like death,
And felt the wind buffet her face with brine
Hard, and harsh thought on thought in long bleak roll
Blown by keen gusts of memory sad as thine
Heap the weight up of pain, and break, and leave
Strength scarce enough to grieve
In the sick heavy spirit, unmanned with strife
Of waves that beat at the tired lips of life.

Nay, sad may be man's memory, sad may be
The dream he weaves him as for shadow of thee,
But scarce one breathing-space, one heartbeat long,
Wilt thou take shadow of sadness on thy song.
Not thou, being more than man or man's desire,
Being bird and God in one,
With throat of gold and spirit of the sun;
The sun whom all our souls and songs call sire,
Whose godhead gave thee, chosen of all our quire,
Thee only of all that serve, of all that sing
Before our sire and king,
Borne up some space on time's world-wandering wing,
This gift, this doom, to bear till time's wing tire--
Life everlasting of eternal fire.

Thee only of all; yet can no memory say
How many a night and day
My heart has been as thy heart, and my life
As thy life is, a sleepless hidden thing,

Full of the thirst and hunger of winter and spring,
That seeks its food not in such love or strife
As fill men's hearts with passionate hours and rest.
From no loved lips and on no loving breast
Have I sought ever for such gifts as bring
Comfort, to stay the secret soul with sleep.
The joys, the loves, the labours, whence men reap
Rathe fruit of hopes and fears,
I have made not mine; the best of all my days
Have been as those fair fruitless summer strays,
Those water-waifs that but the sea-wind steers,
Flakes of glad foam or flowers on footless ways
That take the wind in season and the sun,
And when the wind wills is their season done.

For all my days as all thy days from birth
My heart as thy heart was in me as thee,
Fire; and not all the fountains of the sea
Have waves enough to quench it, nor on earth
Is fuel enough to feed,
While day sows night and night sows day for seed.

We were not marked for sorrow, thou nor I,
For joy nor sorrow, sister, were we made,
To take delight and grief to live and die,
Assuaged by pleasures or by pains affrayed
That melt men's hearts and alter; we retain
A memory mastering pleasure and all pain,
A spirit within the sense of ear and eye,
A soul behind the soul, that seeks and sings
And makes our life move only with its wings
And feed but from its lips, that in return
Feed of our hearts wherein the old fires that burn
Have strength not to consume
Nor glory enough to exalt us past our doom.

Ah, ah, the doom (thou knowest whence rang that wail)
Of the shrill nightingale!
(From whose wild lips, thou knowest, that wail was thrown)
For round about her have the great gods cast
A wing-borne body, and clothed her close and fast
With a sweet life that hath no part in moan.
But me, for me (how hadst thou heart to hear?)
Remains a sundering with the two-edged spear.

Ah, for her doom! so cried in presage then
The bodeful bondslave of the king of men,
And might not win her will.

Too close the entangling dragnet woven of crime,
The snare of ill new-born of elder ill,
The curse of new time for an elder time,
Had caught, and held her yet,
Enmeshed intolerably in the intolerant net,
Who thought with craft to mock the God most high,
And win by wiles his crown of prophecy
From the Sun's hand sublime,
As God were man, to spare or to forget.

But thou,--the gods have given thee and forgiven thee
More than our master gave
That strange-eyed spirit-wounded strange-tongued slave
There questing houndlike where the roofs red-wet
Reeked as a wet red grave.
Life everlasting has their strange grace given thee,
Even hers whom thou wast wont to sing and serve
With eyes, but not with song, too swift to swerve;
Yet might not even thine eyes estranged estrange her,
Who seeing thee too, but inly, burn and bleed
Like that pale princess-priest of Priam's seed,
For stranger service gave thee guerdon stranger;
If this indeed be guerdon, this indeed
Her mercy, this thy meed--
That thou, being more than all we born, being higher
Than all heads crowned of him that only gives
The light whereby man lives,
The bay that bids man moved of God's desire
Lay hand on lute or lyre,
Set lip to trumpet or deflowered green reed--
If this were given thee for a grace indeed,
That thou, being first of all these, thou alone
Shouldst have the grace to die not, but to live
And lose nor change one pulse of song, one tone
Of all that were thy lady's and thine own,
Thy lady's whom thou criedst on to forgive,
Thou, priest and sacrifice on the altar-stone
Where none may worship not of all that live,
Love's priestess, errant on dark ways diverse;
If this were grace indeed for Love to give,
If this indeed were blessing and no curse.

Love's priestess, mad with pain and joy of song,
Song's priestess, mad with joy and pain of love,
Name above all names that are lights above,
We have loved, praised, pitied, crowned and done thee wrong,
O thou past praise and pity; thou the sole
Utterly deathless, perfect only and whole

Immortal, body and soul.
For over all whom time hath overpast
The shadow of sleep inexorable is cast,
The implacable sweet shadow of perfect sleep
That gives not back what life gives death to keep;
Yea, all that lived and loved and sang and sinned
Are all borne down death's cold sweet soundless wind
That blows all night and knows not whom its breath,
Darkling, may touch to death:
But one that wind hath touched and changed not,--one
Whose body and soul are parcel of the sun;
One that earth's fire could burn not, nor the sea
Quench; nor might human doom take hold on thee;
All praise, all pity, all dreams have done thee wrong,
All love, with eyes love-blinded from above;
Song's priestess, mad with joy and pain of love,
Love's priestess, mad with pain and joy of song.

Hast thou none other answer then for me
Than the air may have of thee,
Or the earth's warm woodlands girdling with green girth
Thy secret sleepless burning life on earth,
Or even the sea that once, being woman crowned
And girt with fire and glory of anguish round,
Thou wert so fain to seek to, fain to crave
If she would hear thee and save
And give thee comfort of thy great green grave?
Because I have known thee always who thou art,
Thou knowest, have known thee to thy heart's own heart,
Nor ever have given light ear to storied song
That did thy sweet name sweet unwitting wrong,
Nor ever have called thee nor would call for shame,
Thou knowest, but inly by thine only name,
Sappho--because I have known thee and loved, hast thou
None other answer now?
As brother and sister were we, child and bird,
Since thy first Lesbian word
Flamed on me, and I knew not whence I knew
This was the song that struck my whole soul through,
Pierced my keen spirit of sense with edge more keen,
Even when I knew not,--even ere sooth was seen,--
When thou wast but the tawny sweet winged thing
Whose cry was but of spring.

And yet even so thine ear should hear me--yea,
Hear me this nightfall by this northland bay,
Even for their sake whose loud good word I had,
Singing of thee in the all-beloved clime

Once, where the windy wine of spring makes mad
Our sisters of Majano, who kept time
Clear to my choral rhyme.
Yet was the song acclaimed of these aloud
Whose praise had made mute humbleness misproud,
The song with answering song applauded thus,
But of that Daulian dream of Itylus.
So but for love's love haply was it--nay,
How else?--that even their song took my song's part,
For love of love and sweetness of sweet heart,
Or god-given glorious madness of mid May
And heat of heart and hunger and thirst to sing,
Full of the new wine of the wind of spring.

Or if this were not, and it be not sin
To hold myself in spirit of thy sweet kin,
In heart and spirit of song;
If this my great love do thy grace no wrong,
Thy grace that gave me grace to dwell therein;
If thy gods thus be my gods, and their will
Made my song part of thy song--even such part
As man's hath of God's heart--
And my life like as thy life to fulfil;
What have our gods then given us? Ah, to thee,
Sister, much more, much happier than to me,
Much happier things they have given, and more of grace
Than falls to man's light race;
For lighter are we, all our love and pain
Lighter than thine, who knowest of time or place
Thus much, that place nor time
Can heal or hurt or lull or change again
The singing soul that makes his soul sublime
Who hears the far fall of its fire-fledged rhyme
Fill darkness as with bright and burning rain
Till all the live gloom inly glows, and light
Seems with the sound to cleave the core of night.

The singing soul that moves thee, and that moved
When thou wast woman, and their songs divine
Who mixed for Grecian mouths heaven's lyric wine
Fell dumb, fell down reproved
Before one sovereign Lesbian song of thine.
That soul, though love and life had fain held fast,
Wind-winged with fiery music, rose and past
Through the indrawn hollow of earth and heaven and hell,
As through some strait sea-shell
The wide sea's immemorial song,--the sea
That sings and breathes in strange men's ears of thee

How in her barren bride-bed, void and vast,
Even thy soul sang itself to sleep at last.

To sleep? Ah, then, what song is this, that here
Makes all the night one ear,
One ear fulfilled and mad with music, one
Heart kindling as the heart of heaven, to hear
A song more fiery than the awakening sun
Sings, when his song sets fire
To the air and clouds that build the dead night's pyre?
O thou of divers-coloured mind, O thou
Deathless, God's daughter subtle-souled--lo, now,
Now too the song above all songs, in flight
Higher than the day-star's height,
And sweet as sound the moving wings of night!
Thou of the divers-coloured seat--behold,
Her very song of old!--
O deathless, O God's daughter subtle-souled!
That same cry through this boskage overhead
Rings round reiterated,
Palpitates as the last palpitated,
The last that panted through her lips and died
Not down this grey north sea's half sapped cliff-side
That crumbles toward the coastline, year by year
More near the sands and near;
The last loud lyric fiery cry she cried,
Heard once on heights Leucadian,--heard not here.

Not here; for this that fires our northland night,
This is the song that made
Love fearful, even the heart of love afraid,
With the great anguish of its great delight.
No swan-song, no far-fluttering half-drawn breath,
No word that love of love's sweet nature saith,
No dirge that lulls the narrowing lids of death,
No healing hymn of peace-prevented strife,--
This is her song of life.

I loved thee,--hark, one tenderer note than all--
Atthis, of old time, once--one low long fall,
Sighing--one long low lovely loveless call,
Dying--one pause in song so flamelike fast--
Atthis, long since in old time overpast--
One soft first pause and last.
One,--then the old rage of rapture's fieriest rain
Storms all the music-maddened night again.

Child of God, close craftswoman, I beseech thee,

Bid not ache nor agony break nor master,
Lady, my spirit--
O thou her mistress, might her cry not reach thee?
Our Lady of all men's loves, could Love go past her,
Pass, and not hear it?

She hears not as she heard not; hears not me,
O treble-natured mystery,--how should she
Hear, or give ear?--who heard and heard not thee;
Heard, and went past, and heard not; but all time
Hears all that all the ravin of his years
Hath cast not wholly out of all men's ears
And dulled to death with deep dense funeral chime
Of their reiterate rhyme.
And now of all songs uttering all her praise,
All hers who had thy praise and did thee wrong,
Abides one song yet of her lyric days,
Thine only, this thy song.

O soul triune, woman and god and bird,
Man, man at least has heard.
All ages call thee conqueror, and thy cry
The mightiest as the least beneath the sky
Whose heart was ever set to song, or stirred
With wind of mounting music blown more high
Than wildest wing may fly,
Hath heard or hears,--even Æschylus as I.
But when thy name was woman, and thy word
Human,--then haply, surely then meseems
This thy bird's note was heard on earth of none,
Of none save only in dreams.
In all the world then surely was but one
Song; as in heaven at highest one sceptred sun
Regent, on earth here surely without fail
One only, one imperious nightingale.
Dumb was the field, the woodland mute, the lawn
Silent; the hill was tongueless as the vale
Even when the last fair waif of cloud that felt
Its heart beneath the colouring moonrays melt,
At high midnoon of midnight half withdrawn,
Bared all the sudden deep divine moondawn.
Then, unsaluted by her twin-born tune,
That latter timeless morning of the moon
Rose past its hour of moonrise; clouds gave way
To the old reconquering ray,
But no song answering made it more than day;
No cry of song by night
Shot fire into the cloud-constraining light.

One only, one Æolian island heard
Thrill, but through no bird's throat,
In one strange manlike maiden's godlike note,
The song of all these as a single bird.
Till the sea's portal was as funeral gate
For that sole singer in all time's ageless date
Singled and signed for so triumphal fate,
All nightingales but one in all the world
All her sweet life were silent; only then,
When her life's wing of womanhood was furled,
Their cry, this cry of thine was heard again,
As of me now, of any born of men.
Through sleepless clear spring nights filled full of thee,
Rekindled here, thy ruling song has thrilled
The deep dark air and subtle tender sea
And breathless hearts with one bright sound fulfilled.
Or at midnoon to me
Swimming, and birds about my happier head
Skimming, one smooth soft way by water and air,
To these my bright born brethren and to me
Hath not the clear wind borne or seemed to bear
A song wherein all earth and heaven and sea
Were molten in one music made of thee
To enforce us, O our sister of the shore,
Look once in heart back landward and adore?
For songless were we sea-mews, yet had we
More joy than all things joyful of thee--more,
Haply, than all things happiest; nay, save thee,
In thy strong rapture of imperious joy
Too high for heart of sea-borne bird or boy,
What living things were happiest if not we?
But knowing not love nor change nor wrath nor wrong,
No more we knew of song.

Song, and the secrets of it, and their might,
What blessings curse it and what curses bless,
I know them since my spirit had first in sight,
Clear as thy song's words or the live sun's light,
The small dark body's Lesbian loveliness
That held the fire eternal; eye and ear
Were as a god's to see, a god's to hear,
Through all his hours of daily and nightly chime,
The sundering of the two-edged spear of time:
The spear that pierces even the sevenfold shields
Of mightiest Memory, mother of all songs made,
And wastes all songs as roseleaves kissed and frayed
As here the harvest of the foam-flowered fields;
But thine the spear may waste not that he wields

Since first the God whose soul is man's live breath,
The sun whose face hath our sun's face for shade,
Put all the light of life and love and death
Too strong for life, but not for love too strong,
Where pain makes peace with pleasure in thy song,
And in thine heart, where love and song make strife,
Fire everlasting of eternal life.

THE GARDEN OF CYMODOCE

Sea, and bright wind, and heaven of ardent air,
More dear than all things earth-born; O to me
Mother more dear than love's own longing, sea,
More than love's eyes are, fair,
Be with my spirit of song as wings to bear,
As fire to feel and breathe and brighten; be
A spirit of sense more deep of deity,
A light of love, if love may be, more strong
In me than very song.
For song I have loved with second love, but thee,
Thee first, thee, mother; ere my songs had breath,
That love of loves, whose bondage makes man free,
Was in me strong as death.
And seeing no slave may love thee, no, not one
That loves not freedom more,
And more for thy sake loves her, and for hers
Thee; or that hates not, on whate'er thy shore
Or what thy wave soever, all things done
Of man beneath the sun
In his despite and thine, to cross and curse
Your light and song that as with lamp and verse
Guide safe the strength of our sphered universe,
Thy breath it was, thou knowest, and none but thine,
That taught me love of one thing more divine.

Ah, yet my youth was old   [Strophe 1.
Its first years dead and cold
As last year's autumn's gold,
And all my spirit of singing sick and sad and sere,
Or ever I might behold
The fairest of thy fold
Engirt, enringed, enrolled,
In all thy flower-sweet flock of islands dear and near.

Yet in my heart I deemed   [Strophe 2.
The fairest things, meseemed,

Truth, dreaming, ever dreamed,
Had made mine eyes already like a god's to see:
Of all sea-things that were
Clothed on with water and air,
That none could live more fair
Than thy sweet love long since had shown for love to me.

I knew not, mother of mine,   [Antistrophe 1.
That one birth more divine
Than all births else of thine
That hang like flowers or jewels on thy deep soft breast
Was left for me to shine
Above thy girdling line
Of bright and breathing brine,
To take mine eyes with rapture and my sense with rest.

That this was left for me,   [Antistrophe 2.
Mother, to have of thee,
To touch, to taste, to see,
To feel as fire fulfilling all my blood and breath,
As wine of living fire
Keen as the heart's desire
That makes the heart its pyre
And on its burning visions burns itself to death.

For here of all thy waters, here of all
Thy windy ways the wildest, and beset
As some beleaguered city's war-breached wall
With deaths enmeshed all round it in deep net,
Thick sown with rocks deadlier than steel, and fierce
With loud cross-countering currents, where the ship
Flags, flickering like a wind-bewildered leaf,
The densest weft of waves that prow may pierce
Coils round the sharpest warp of shoals that dip
Suddenly, scarce well under for one brief
Keen breathing-space between the streams adverse,
Scarce showing the fanged edge of one hungering lip
Or one tooth lipless of the ravening reef;
And midmost of the murderous water's web
All round it stretched and spun,
Laughs, reckless of rough tide and raging ebb,
The loveliest thing that shines against the sun.

O flower of all wind-flowers and sea-flowers,   [Strophe 3.
Made lovelier by love of the sea
Than thy golden own field-flowers, or tree-flowers
Like foam of the sea-facing tree!
No foot but the seamew's there settles

On the spikes of thine anthers like horns,
With snow-coloured spray for thy petals,
Black rocks for thy thorns.

Was it here, in the waste of his waters,   [Antistrophe 3.
That the lordly north wind, when his love
On the fairest of many king's daughters
Bore down for a spoil from above,
Chose forth of all farthest far islands
As a haven to harbour her head,
Of all lowlands on earth and all highlands,
His bride-worthy bed?

Or haply, my sea-flower, he found thee   [Strophe 4.
Made fast as with anchors to land,
And broke, that his waves might be round thee,
Thy fetters like rivets of sand?
And afar by the blast of him drifted
Thy blossom of beauty was borne,
As a lark by the heart in her lifted
To mix with the morn?

By what rapture of rage, by what vision   [Antistrophe 4.
Of a heavenlier heaven than above,
Was he moved to devise thy division
From the land as a rest for his love?
As a nest when his wings would remeasure
The ways where of old they would be,
As a bride-bed upbuilt for his pleasure
By sea-rock and sea?

For in no deeps of midmost inland May
More flowerbright flowers the hawthorn, or more sweet
Swells the wild gold of the earth for wandering feet;
For on no northland way
Crowds the close whin-bloom closer, set like thee
With thorns about for fangs of sea-rock shown
Through blithe lips of the bitter brine to lee;
Nor blithelier landward comes the sea-wind blown,
Nor blithelier leaps the land-wind back to sea:
Nor louder springs the living song of birds
To shame our sweetest words.
And in the narrowest of thine hollowest hold
For joy thine aspens quiver as though for cold,
And many a self-lit flower-illumined tree
Outlaughs with snowbright or with rosebright glee
The laughter of the fields whose laugh is gold.
Yea, even from depth to height,

Even thine own beauty with its own delight
Fulfils thine heart in thee an hundredfold
Beyond the larger hearts of islands bright
With less intense contraction of desire
Self-satiate, centred in its own deep fire;
Of shores not self-enchanted and entranced
By heavenly severance from all shadow of mirth
Or mourning upon earth:
As thou, by no similitude enhanced,
By no fair foil made fairer, but alone
Fair as could be no beauty save thine own,
And wondrous as no world-beholden wonder:
Throned, with the world's most perilous sea for throne,
And praised from all its choral throats of thunder.

Yet one praise hast thou, holier   [Strophe 5.
Than praise of theirs may be,
To exalt thee, wert thou lowlier
Than all that take the sea
With shores whence waves ebb slowlier
Than these fall off from thee;

That One, whose name gives glory,   [Antistrophe 5.
One man whose life makes light,
One crowned and throned in story
Above all empire's height,
Came, where thy straits run hoary,
To hold thee fast in sight;

With hallowing eyes to hold thee,   [Strophe 6.
With rapturous heart to read,
To encompass and enfold thee
With love whence all men feed,
To brighten and behold thee,
Who is mightiest of man's seed:

More strong than strong disaster,   [Antistrophe 6.
For fate and fear too strong;
Earth's friend, whose eyes look past her,
Whose hands would purge of wrong;
Our lord, our light, our master,
Whose word sums up all song.

Be it April or September   [Strophe 7.
That plays his perfect part,
Burn June or blow December,
Thou canst not in thine heart
But rapturously remember,

All heavenlike as thou art,

Whose footfall made thee fairer,   [Antistrophe 7.
Whose passage more divine,
Whose hand, our thunder-bearer,
Held fire that bade thee shine
With subtler glory and rarer
Than thrills the sun's own shrine.

Who knows how then his godlike banished gaze
Turned haply from its goal of natural days
And homeward hunger for the clear French clime,
Toward English earth, whereunder now the Accursed
Rots, in the hate of all men's hearts inhearsed,
A carrion ranker to the sense of time
For that sepulchral gift of stone and lime
By royal grace laid on it, less of weight
Than the load laid by fate,
Fate, misbegotten child of his own crime,
Son of as foul a bastard-bearing birth
As even his own on earth;
Less heavy than the load of cursing piled
By loyal grace of all souls undefiled
On one man's head, whose reeking soul made rotten
The loathed live corpse on earth once misbegotten?
But when our Master's homeless feet were here
France yet was foul with joy more foul than fear,
And slavery chosen, more vile by choice of chance
Than dull damnation of inheritance
From Russian year to year
Alas fair mother of men, alas my France,
What ailed thee so to fall, that wert so dear
For all men's sake to all men, in such trance,
Plague-stricken? Had the very Gods, that saw
Thy glory lighten on us for a law,
Thy gospel go before us for a guide,
Had these waxed envious of our love and awe,
Or was it less their envy than thy pride
That bared thy breast for the obscene vulture-claw,
High priestess, by whose mouth Love prophesied
That fate should yet mean freedom? Howsoever,
That hour, the helper of men's hearts, we praise,
Which blots out of man's book of after days
The name above all names abhorred for ever.
And His name shall we praise not, whom these flowers,
These rocks and ravening waters bound for girth
Round this wild starry spanlong plot of earth,
Beheld, the mightier for those heavier hours

That bowed his heart not down
Nor marred one crowning blossom of his crown?
For surely, might we say,
Even from the dark deep sea-gate that makes way
Through channelled darkness for the darkling day
Hardly to let men's faltering footfall win
The sunless passage in,
Where breaks a world aflower against the sun,
A small sweet world of wave-encompassed wonder
Kept from the wearier landward world asunder
With violence of wild waters, and with thunder
Of many winds as one,
To where the keen sea-current grinds and frets
The black bright sheer twin flameless Altarlets
That lack no live blood-sacrifice they crave
Of shipwreck and the shrine-subservient wave,
Having for priest the storm-wind, and for choir
Lightnings and clouds whose prayer and praise are fire,
All the isle acclaimed him coming; she, the least
Of all things loveliest that the sea's love hides
From strange men's insult, walled about with tides
That bid strange guests back from her flower-strewn feast,
Set all her fields aflower, her flowers aflame,
To applaud him that he came.
Nor surely flashed not something of delight
Through that steep strait of rock whose twin-cliffed height
Links crag with crag reiterate, land with land,
By one sheer thread of narrowing precipice
Bifront, that binds and sunders
Abyss from hollower imminent abyss
And wilder isle with island, blind for bliss
Of sea that lightens and of wind that thunders;
Nor pealed not surely back from deep to steep
Reverberate acclamation, steep to deep
Inveterately reclaiming and replying
Praise, and response applausive; nor the sea,
For all the sea-wind's crying,
Knew not the song her sister, even as she
Thundering, or like her confluent spring-tides brightening,
And like her darkness lightening;
The song that moved about him silent, now
Both soundless wings refolded and refurled
On that Promethean brow,
Then quivering as for flight that wakes the world.

From the roots of the rocks underlying the gulfs that engird it around   **[Strophe 8.**
Was the isle not enkindled with light of him landing, or thrilled not with sound?
Yea, surely the sea like a harper laid hand on the shore as a lyre,

As the lyre in his own for a birthright of old that was given of his sire,
And the hand of the child was put forth on the chords yet alive and aflame
From the hand of the God that had wrought it in heaven; and the hand was the same.
And the tongue of the child spake, singing; and never a note that he sang,
But the strings made answer unstricken, as though for the God they rang.
And the eyes of the child shone, lightening; and touched as by life at his nod,
They shuddered with music, and quickened as though from the glance of the God.
So trembled the heart of the hills and the rocks to receive him, and yearned
With desirous delight of his presence and love that beholding him burned.
Yea, down through the mighty twin hollows where never the sunlight shall be,
Deep sunk under imminent earth, and subdued to the stress of the sea,
That feel when the dim week changes by change of their tides in the dark,
As the wave sinks under within them, reluctant, removed from its mark,
Even there in the terror of twilight in bloom with its blossoms ablush,
Did a sense of him touch not the gleam of their flowers with a fierier flush?
Though the sun they behold not for ever, yet knew they not over them One
Whose soul was the soul of the morning, whose song was the song of the sun?
But the secrets inviolate of sunlight in hollows untrodden of day,
Shall he dream what are these who beholds not? or he that hath seen, shall he say?
For the path is for passage of sea-mews; and he that hath glided and leapt
Over sea-grass and sea-rock, alighting as one from a citadel crept
That his foemen beleaguer, descending by darkness and stealth, at the last
Peers under, and all is as hollow to hellward, agape and aghast.
But afloat and afar in the darkness a tremulous colour subsides   **[Antistrophe 8.**
From the crimson high crest of the purple-peaked roof to the soft-coloured sides
That brighten as ever they widen till downward the level is won
Of the soundless and colourless water that knows not the sense of the sun:
From the crown of the culminant arch to the floor of the lakelet abloom,
One infinite blossom of blossoms innumerable aflush through the gloom.
All under the deeps of the darkness are glimmering; all over impends
An immeasurable infinite flower of the dark that dilates and descends,
That exults and expands in its breathless and blind efflorescence of heart
As it broadens and bows to the wave-ward, and breathes not, and hearkens apart.
As a beaker inverse at a feast on Olympus, exhausted of wine,
But inlaid as with rose from the lips of Dione that left it divine:
From the lips everliving of laughter and love everlasting, that leave
In the cleft of his heart who shall kiss them a snake to corrode it and cleave.
So glimmers the gloom into glory, the glory recoils into gloom,
That the eye of the sun could not kindle, the lip not of Love could relume.
So darkens reverted the cup that the kiss of her mouth set on fire:
So blackens a brand in his eyeshot asmoulder awhile from the pyre.
For the beam from beneath and without it refrangent again from the wave
Strikes up through the portal a ghostly reverse on the dome of the cave,
On the depth of the dome ever darkling and dim to the crown of its arc:
That the sun-coloured tapestry, sunless for ever, may soften the dark.
But within through the side-seen archway a glimmer again from the right
Is the seal of the sea's tide set on the mouth of the mystery of night.
And the seal on the seventh day breaks but a little, that man by its mean

May behold what the sun hath not looked on, the stars of the night have not seen.

Even like that hollow-bosomed rose, inverse
And infinite, the heaven of thy vast verse,
Our Master, over all our souls impends,
Imminent; we, with heart-enkindled eyes
Upwondering, search the music-moulded skies
Sphere by sweet sphere, concordant as it blends
Light of bright sound, sound of clear light, in one,
As all the stars found utterance through the sun.
And all that heaven is like a rose in bloom,
Flower-coloured, where its own sun's fires illume
As from one central and imperious heart
The whole sky's every part:
But lightening still and darkling downward, lo
The light and darkness of it,
The leaping of the lamping levin afar
Between the full moon and the sunset star,
The war-song of the sounding skies aglow,
That have the herald thunder for their prophet:
From north to south the lyric lights that leap,
The tragic sundawns reddening east and west
As with bright blood from one Promethean breast,
The peace of noon that strikes the sea to sleep,
The wail over the world of all that weep,
The peace of night when death brings life on rest.

Goddess who gatherest all the herded waves
Into thy great sweet pastureless green fold,
Even for our love of old,
I pray thee by thy power that slays and saves,
Take thou my song of this thy flower to keep
Who hast my heart in hold;
And from thine high place of thy garden-steep,
Where one sheer terrace oversees thy deep
From the utmost rock-reared height
Down even to thy dear depths of night and light,
Take my song's salutation; and on me
Breathe back the benediction of thy sea.

Between two seas the sea-bird's wing makes halt,
Wind-weary; while with lifting head he waits
For breath to reinspire him from the gates
That open still toward sunrise on the vault
High-domed of morning, and in flight's default
With spreading sense of spirit anticipates
What new sea now may lure beyond the straits
His wings exulting that her winds exalt

And fill them full as sails to seaward spread,
Fulfilled with fair speed's promise. Pass, my song,
Forth to the haven of thy desire and dread,
The presence of our lord, long loved and long
Far off above beholden, who to thee
Was as light kindling all a windy sea.

BIRTHDAY ODE

FOR THE ANNIVERSARY FESTIVAL OF VICTOR HUGO, FEBRUARY 26, 1880

Spring, born in heaven ere many a springtime flown,   [Strophe 1.
Dead spring that sawest on earth
A babe of deathless birth,
A flower of rosier flowerage than thine own,
A glory of goodlier godhead; even this day,
That floods the mist of February with May,
And strikes death dead with sunlight, and the breath
Whereby the deadly doers are done to death,
They that in day's despite
Would crown the imperial night,
And in deep hate of insubmissive spring
Rethrone the royal winter for a king,
This day that casts the days of darkness down
Low as a broken crown,
We call thee from the gulf of deeds and days,
Deathless and dead, to hear us whom we praise.

A light of many lights about thine head,   [Antistrophe 1.
Lights manifold and one,
Stars molten in a sun,
A sun of divers beams incorporated,
Compact of confluent aureoles, each more fair
Than man, save only at highest of man, may wear,
So didst thou rise, when this our grey-grown age
Had trod two paces of his pilgrimage,
Two paces through the gloom
From his fierce father's tomb,
Led by cross lights of lightnings, and the flame
That burned in darkness round one darkling name;
So didst thou rise, nor knewest thy glory, O thou
Re-risen upon us now,
The glory given thee for a grace to give,
And take the praise of all men's hearts that live.

First in the dewy ray   [Epode 1.

Ere dawn be slain of day
The fresh crowned lilies of discrowned kings' prime
Sprang splendid as of old
With moonlight-coloured gold
And rays refract from the oldworld heaven of time;
Pale with proud light of stars decreased
In westward wane reluctant from the conquering east.

But even between their golden olden bloom   [Strophe 2.
Strange flowers of wildwood glory,
With frost and moonshine hoary,
Thrust up the new growths of their green-leaved gloom,
Red buds of ballad blossom, where the dew
Blushed as with bloodlike passion, and its hue
Was as the life and love of hearts on flame,
And fire from forth of each live chalice came:
Young sprays of elder song,
Stem straight and petal strong,
Bright foliage with dark frondage overlaid,
And light the lovelier for its lordlier shade;
And morn and even made loud in woodland lone
With cheer of clarions blown,
And through the tournay's clash and clarion's cheer
Laugh to laugh echoing, tear washed off by tear.

Then eastward far past northland lea and lawn
Beneath a heavier light   [Antistrophe 2.
Of stormier day and night
Began the music of the heaven of dawn;
Bright sound of battle along the Grecian waves,
Loud light of thunder above the Median graves,
New strife, new song on Æschylean seas,
Canaris risen above Themistocles;
Old glory of warrior ghosts
Shed fresh on filial hosts,
With dewfall redder than the dews of day,
And earth-born lightnings out of bloodbright spray;
Then through the flushed grey gloom on shadowy sheaves
Low flights of falling leaves;
And choirs of birds transfiguring as they throng
All the world's twilight and the soul's to song.

Voices more dimly deep   [Epode 2.
Than the inmost heart of sleep,
And tenderer than the rose-mouthed morning's lips;
And midmost of them heard
The viewless water's word,
The sea's breath in the wind's wing and the ship's,

That bids one swell and sound and smite
And rend that other in sunder as with fangs by night.

But ah! the glory of shadow and mingling ray,   [Strophe 3.
The story of morn and even
Whose tale was writ in heaven
And had for scroll the night, for scribe the day!
For scribe the prophet of the morning, far
Exalted over twilight and her star;
For scroll beneath his Apollonian hand
The dim twin wastes of sea and glimmering land.
Hark, on the hill-wind, clear
For all men's hearts to hear
Sound like a stream at nightfall from the steep
That all time's depths might answer, deep to deep,
With trumpet-measures of triumphal wail
From windy vale to vale,
The crying of one for love that strayed and sinned
Whose brain took madness of the mountain wind.

Between the birds of brighter and duskier wing,   [Antistrophe 3.
What mightier-moulded forms
Girt with red clouds and storms
Mix their strong hearts with theirs that soar and sing?
Before the storm-blast blown of death's dark horn
The marriage moonlight withers, that the morn
For two made one may find three made by death
One ruin at the blasting of its breath:
Clothed with heart's flame renewed
And strange new maidenhood,
Faith lightens on the lips that bloomed for hire
Pure as the lightning of love's first-born fire:
Wide-eyed and patient ever, till the curse
Find where to fall and pierce,
Keen expiation whets with edge more dread
A father's wrong to smite a father's head.

Borgia, supreme from birth   [Epode 3.
As loveliest born on earth
Since earth bore ever women that were fair;
Scarce known of her own house
If daughter or sister or spouse;
Who holds men's hearts yet helpless with her hair;
The direst of divine things made,
Bows down her amorous aureole half suffused with shade.

As red the fire-scathed royal northland bloom,   [Strophe 4.
That left our story a name

Dyed through with blood and flame
Ere her life shrivelled from a fierier doom
Than theirs her priests bade pass from earth in fire
To slake the thirst of God their Lord's desire:
As keen the blast of love-enkindled fate
That burst the Paduan tyrant's guarded gate:
As sad the softer moan
Made one with music's own
For one whose feet made music as they fell
On ways by loveless love made hot from hell:
But higher than these and all the song thereof
The perfect heart of love,
The heart by fraud and hate once crucified,
That, dying, gave thanks, and in thanksgiving died.

Above the windy walls that rule the Rhine   [Antistrophe 4.
A noise of eagles' wings
And wintry war-time rings,
With roar of ravage trampling corn and vine
And storm of wrathful wassail dashed with song,
And under these the watch of wreakless wrong,
With fire of eyes anhungered; and above
These, the light of the stricken eyes of love,
The faint sweet eyes that follow
The wind-outwinging swallow,
And face athirst with young wan yearning mouth
Turned after toward the unseen all-golden south,
Hopeless to see the birds back ere life wane,
Or the leaves born again;
And still the might and music mastering fate
Of life more strong than death and love than hate.

In spectral strength biform   [Epode 4.
Stand the twin sons of storm
Transfigured by transmission of one hand
That gives the new-born time
Their semblance more sublime
Than once it lightened over each man's land;
There Freedom's winged and wide-mouthed hound,
And here our high Dictator, in his son discrowned.

What strong-limbed shapes of kindred throng round these   [Strophe 5.
Before, between, behind,
Sons born of one man's mind,
Fed at his hands and fostered round his knees?
Fear takes the spirit in thraldom at his nod,
And pity makes it as the spirit of God,
As his own soul that from her throne above

Sheds on all souls of men her showers of love,
On all earth's evil and pain
Pours mercy forth as rain
And comfort as the dewfall on dry land;
And feeds with pity from a faultless hand
All by their own fault stricken, all cast out
By all men's scorn or doubt,
Or with their own hands wounded, or by fate
Brought into bondage of men's fear or hate.

In violence of strange visions north and south   [Antistrophe 5.
Confronted, east and west,
With frozen or fiery breast,
Eyes fixed or fevered, pale or bloodred mouth,
Kept watch about his dawn-enkindled dreams;
But ere high noon a light of nearer beams
Made his young heaven of manhood more benign,
And love made soft his lips with spiritual wine,
And left them fired, and fed
With sacramental bread,
And sweet with honey of tenderer words than tears
To feed men's hopes and fortify men's fears,
And strong to silence with benignant breath
The lips that doom to death,
And swift with speech like fire in fiery lands
To melt the steel's edge in the headsman's hands.

Higher than they rose of old,   [Epode 5.
New builded now, behold,
The live great likeness of Our Lady's towers;
And round them like a dove
Wounded, and sick with love,
One fair ghost moving, crowned with fateful flowers,
Watched yet with eyes of bloodred lust
And eyes of love's heart broken and unbroken trust.

But sadder always under shadowier skies,   [Strophe 6.
More pale and sad and clear
Waxed always, drawn more near,
The face of Duty lit with Love's own eyes;
Till the awful hands that culled in rosier hours
From fairy-footed fields of wild old flowers
And sorcerous woods of Rhineland, green and hoary,
Young children's chaplets of enchanted story,
The great kind hands that showed
Exile its homeward road,
And, as man's helper made his foeman God,
Of pity and mercy wrought themselves a rod,

And opened for Napoleon's wandering kin
France, and bade enter in,
And threw for all the doors of refuge wide,
Took to them lightning in the thunder-tide.

For storm on earth above had risen from under,
Out of the hollow of hell,   [Antistrophe 6.
Such storm as never fell
From darkest deeps of heaven distract with thunder;
A cloud of cursing, past all shape of thought,
More foul than foulest dreams, and overfraught
With all obscene things and obscure of birth
That ever made infection of man's earth;
Having all hell for cloak
Wrapped round it as a smoke
And in its womb such offspring so defiled
As earth bare never for her loathliest child,
Rose, brooded, reddened, broke, and with its breath
Put France to poisonous death;
Yea, far as heaven's red labouring eye could glance,
France was not, save in men cast forth of France.

Then,--while the plague-sore grew   [Epode 6.
Two darkling decades through,
And rankled in the festering flesh of time,--
Where darkness binds and frees
The wildest of wild seas
In fierce mutations of the unslumbering clime,
There, sleepless too, o'er shuddering wrong
One hand appointed shook the reddening scourge of song.

And through the lightnings of the apparent word
Dividing shame's dense night   [Strophe 7.
Sounds lovelier than the light
And light more sweet than song from night's own bird
Mixed each their hearts with other, till the gloom
Was glorious as with all the stars in bloom,
Sonorous as with all the spheres in chime
Heard far through flowering heaven: the sea, sublime
Once only with its own
Old winds' and waters' tone,
Sad only or glad with its own glory, and crowned
With its own light, and thrilled with its own sound,
Learnt now their song, more sweet than heaven's may be,
Who pass away by sea;
The song that takes of old love's land farewell,
With pulse of plangent water like a knell.

And louder ever and louder and yet more loud
Till night be shamed of morn
Rings the Black Huntsman's horn
Through darkening deeps beneath the covering cloud,
Till all the wild beasts of the darkness hear;
Till the Czar quake, till Austria cower for fear,
Till the king breathe not, till the priest wax pale,
Till spies and slayers on seats of judgment quail,
Till mitre and cowl bow down
And crumble as a crown,
Till Cæsar driven to lair and hounded Pope
Reel breathless and drop heartless out of hope,
And one the uncleanest kinless beast of all
Lower than his fortune fall;
The wolfish waif of casual empire, born
To turn all hate and horror cold with scorn.

[Antistrophe 7.

Yea, even at night's full noon
Light's birth-song brake in tune,
Spake, witnessing that with us one must be,
God; naming so by name
That priests have brought to shame
The strength whose scourge sounds on the smitten sea;
The mystery manifold of might
Which bids the wind give back to night the things of night.

[Epode 7.

Even God, the unknown of all time; force or thought,
Nature or fate or will,
Clothed round with good and ill,
Veiled and revealed of all things and of nought,
Hooded and helmed with mystery, girt and shod
With light and darkness, unapparent God.
Him the high prophet o'er his wild work bent
Found indivisible ever and immanent
At hidden heart of truth,
In forms of age and youth
Transformed and transient ever; masked and crowned,
From all bonds loosened and with all bonds bound,
Diverse and one with all things; love and hate,
Earth, and the starry state
Of heaven immeasurable, and years that flee
As clouds and winds and rays across the sea.

[Strophe 8.

But higher than stars and deeper than the waves
Of day and night and morrow
That roll for all time, sorrow
Keeps ageless watch over perpetual graves.
From dawn to morning of the soul in flower,

[Antistrophe 8.

Through toils and dreams and visions, to that hour
When all the deeps were opened, and one doom
Took two sweet lives to embrace them and entomb,
The strong song plies its wing
That makes the darkness ring
And the deep light reverberate sound as deep;
Song soft as flowers or grass more soft than sleep,
Song bright as heaven above the mounting bird,
Song like a God's tears heard
Falling, fulfilled of life and death and light,
And all the stars and all the shadow of night.

Till, when its flight hath past   [Epode 8.
Time's loftiest mark and last,
The goal where good kills evil with a kiss,
And Darkness in God's sight
Grows as his brother Light,
And heaven and hell one heart whence all the abyss
Throbs with love's music; from his trance
Love waking leads it home to her who stayed in France.

But now from all the world-old winds of the air   [Strophe 9.
One blast of record rings
As from time's hidden springs
With roar of rushing wings and fires that bear
Toward north and south sonorous, east and west,
Forth of the dark wherein its records rest,
The story told of the ages, writ nor sung
By man's hand ever nor by mortal tongue
Till, godlike with desire,
One tongue of man took fire,
One hand laid hold upon the lightning, one
Rose up to bear time witness what the sun
Had seen, and what the moon and stars of night
Beholding lost not light:
From dawn to dusk what ways man wandering trod
Even through the twilight of the gods to God.

From dawn of man and woman twain and one   [Antistrophe 9.
When the earliest dews impearled
The front of all the world
Ringed with aurorean aureole of the sun,
To days that saw Christ's tears and hallowing breath
Put life for love's sake in the lips of death,
And years as waves whose brine was fire, whose foam
Blood, and the ravage of Neronian Rome;
And the eastern crescent's horn
Mightier awhile than morn;

And knights whose lives were flights of eagles' wings,
And lives like snakes' lives of engendering kings;
And all the ravin of all the swords that reap
Lives cast as sheaves on heap
From all the billowing harvest-fields of fight;
And sounds of love-songs lovelier than the light.

The grim dim thrones of the east   [Epode 9.
Set for death's riotous feast
Round the bright board where darkling centuries wait,
And servile slaughter, mute,
Feeds power with fresh red fruit,
Glitter and groan with mortal food of fate;
And throne and cup and lamp's bright breath
Bear witness to their lord of only night and death.

Dead freedom by live empire lies defiled,   [Strophe 10.
And murder at his feet
Plies lust with wine and meat,
With offering of an old man and a child,
With holy body and blood, inexpiable
Communion in the sacrament of hell,
Till, reeking from their monstrous eucharist,
The lips wax cold that murdered where they kissed,
And empire in mid feast
Fall as a slaughtered beast
Headless, and ease men's hungering hearts of fear
Lest God were none in heaven, to see nor hear,
And purge his own pollution with the flood
Poured of his black base blood
So first found healing, poisonous as it poured;
And on the clouds the archangel cleanse his sword.

As at the word unutterable that made   [Antistrophe 10.
Of day and night division,
From vision on to vision,
From dream to dream, from darkness into shade,
From sunshine into sunlight, moves and lives
The steersman's eye, the helming hand that gives
Life to the wheels and wings that whirl along
The immeasurable impulse of the sphere of song
Through all the eternal years,
Beyond all stars and spheres,
Beyond the washing of the waves of time,
Beyond all heights where no thought else may climb,
Beyond the darkling dust of suns that were,
Past height and depth of air;
And in the abyss whence all things move that are

Finds only living Love, the sovereign star.

Nor less the weight and worth   [Epode 10.
Found even of love on earth
To wash all stain of tears and sins away,
On dying lips alit
That living knew not it,
In the winged shape of song with death to play:
To warm young children with its wings,
And try with fire the heart elect for godlike things.

For all worst wants of all most miserable   [Strophe 11.
With divine hands to deal
All balms and herbs that heal,
Among all woes whereunder poor men dwell
Our Master sent his servant Love, to be
On earth his witness; but the strange deep sea,
Mother of life and death inextricate,
What work should Love do there, to war with fate?
Yet there must Love too keep
At heart of the eyeless deep
Watch, and wage war wide-eyed with all its wonders,
Lower than the lightnings of its waves, and thunders
Of seas less monstrous than the births they bred;
Keep high there heart and head,
And conquer: then for prize of all toils past
Feel the sea close them in again at last.

A day of direr doom arisen thereafter   [Antistrophe 11.
With cloud and fire in strife
Lightens and darkens life
Round one by man's hand masked with living laughter,
A man by men bemonstered, but by love,
Watched with blind eyes as of a wakeful dove,
And wooed by lust, that in her rosy den
As fire on flesh feeds on the souls of men,
To take the intense impure
Burnt-offering of her lure,
Divine and dark and bright and naked, strange
With ravenous thirst of life reversed and change,
As though the very heaven should shrivel and swell
With hunger after hell,
Run mad for dear damnation, and desire
To feel its light thrilled through with stings of fire.

Above a windier sea,   [Epode 11.
The glory of Ninety-three
Fills heaven with blood-red and with rose-red beams

That earth beholding grows
Herself one burning rose
Flagrant and fragrant with strange deeds and dreams,
Dreams dyed as love's own flower, and deeds
Stained as with love's own life-blood, that for love's sake bleeds.

And deeper than all deeps of seas and skies   [Strophe 12.
Wherein the shadows are
Called sun and moon and star
That rapt conjecture metes with mounting eyes,
Loud with strange waves and lustrous with new spheres,
Shines, masked at once and manifest of years,
Shakespeare, a heaven of heavenly eyes beholden;
And forward years as backward years grow golden
With light of deeds and words
And flight of God's fleet birds,
Angels of wrath and love and truth and pity;
And higher on exiled eyes their natural city
Dawns down the depths of vision, more sublime
Than all truths born of time;
And eyes that wept above two dear sons dead
Grow saving stars to guard one hopeless head.

Bright round the brows of banished age had shone   [Antistrophe 12.
In vision flushed with truth
The rosy glory of youth
On streets and woodlands where in days long gone
Sweet love sang light and loud and deep and dear:
And far the trumpets of the dreadful year
Had pealed and wailed in darkness: last arose
The song of children, kindling as a rose
At breath of sunrise, born
Of the red flower of morn
Whose face perfumes deep heaven with odorous light
And thrills all through the wings of souls in flight
Close as the press of children at His knee
Whom if the high priest see,
Dreaming, as homeless on dark earth he trod,
The lips that praise him shall not know for God.

O sovereign spirit, above   [Epode 12.
All offering but man's love,
All praise and prayer and incense undefiled!
The one thing stronger found
Than towers with iron bound;
The one thing lovelier than a little child,
And deeper than the seas are deep,
And tenderer than such tears of love as angels weep.

Dante, the seer of all things evil and good,
Beheld two ladies, Beauty
And high life-hallowing Duty,
That strove for sway upon his mind and mood
And held him in alternating accord
Fast bound at feet of either: but our lord,
The seer and singer of righteousness and wrong
Who stands now master of all the keys of song,
Sees both as dewdrops run
Together in the sun,
For him not twain but one thing twice divine;
Even as his speech and song are bread and wine
For all souls hungering and all hearts athirst
At best of days and worst,
And both one sacrament of Love's great giving
To feed the spirit and sense of all souls living.

The seventh day in the wind's month, ten years gone   [Antistrophe 13.
Since heaven-espousing earth
Gave the Republic birth,
The mightiest soul put mortal raiment on
That came forth singing ever in man's ears
Of all souls with us, and through all these years
Rings yet the lordliest, waxen yet more strong,
That on our souls hath shed itself in song,
Poured forth itself like rain
On souls like springing grain
That with its procreant beams and showers were fed
For living wine and sacramental bread;
Given all itself as air gives life and light,
Utterly, as of right;
The goodliest gift our age hath given, to be
Ours, while the sun gives glory to the sea.

Our Father and Master and Lord,   [Epode 13.
Who hast thy song for sword,
For staff thy spirit, and our hearts for throne:
As in past years of wrong,
Take now my subject song,
To no crowned head made humble but thine own;
That on thy day of worldly birth
Gives thanks for all thou hast given past thanks of all on earth.

Algernon Charles Swinburne – A Short Biography

Algernon Charles Swinburne was born at 7 Chester Street, Grosvenor Place, in London, on April 5th, 1837. He was the eldest of six children born to Captain Charles Henry Swinburne and Lady Jane Henrietta, daughter of the 3rd Earl of Ashburnham, a wealthy Northumbrian family.

Swinburne spent his early years at East Dene in Bonchurch, on the Isle of Wight. As a child, Swinburne was nervous and frail, but also imbued with a nervous energy and fearlessness almost to the point of recklessness.

He was schooled at Eton College from 1849 to 1853. It was here that he first began to write poetry. He excelled at languages and whilst still at Eton won first prizes in both French and Italian.

From Eton he moved to Oxford where he attended at Balliol College from 1856. Here he met friends to whom he became closely attached, among them Dante Gabriel Rossetti, William Morris and Edward Burne-Jones, who in 1857, were painting their Arthurian murals on the walls of the Oxford Union. At Oxford Swinburne was mentored by Benjamin Jowett, the master of Balliol College, who recognised his poetic talent and, intervening on his behalf, tried to keep him from being expelled when he celebrated the Italian patriot Orsini, and his failed attempt on the life of Napoleon III in 1858. Swinburne had to leave the Universcity for a few months due to this but returned in May, 1860 but never received a degree.

Summers were usually spent at Capheaton Hall in Northumberland, the house of his grandfather, Sir John Swinburne, 6th Baronet, who had a famous library and was himself President of the Literary and Philosophical Society in Newcastle upon Tyne.

Swinburne proudly considered himself a native of Northumberland and this is reflected in poems such as the intensely patriotic 'Northumberland' and 'Grace Darling'. He enjoyed riding across the moors and was, it was said, a daring horseman, as he moved 'through honeyed leagues of the northland border', as he remembered the Scottish border in his Recollections.

In the period from 1857 to 1860, Swinburne was one of a number of Pre-Raphaelite's who visited and became part of Lady Pauline Trevelyan's intellectual circle at Wallington Hall, a few miles west of Morpeth in Northumberland.

After leaving college, he moved to London and began his career in earnest as well as becoming a constant visitor to the Rossetti's house. To Rossetti Swinburne was his 'little Northumbrian friend', an affectionate reference to Swinburne's small stature—a mere five foot four. Whatever Swinburne lacked in height he made up for in poetic talent. However, with the burden of such great talent came the unveiling of a dark side that was to cause him pain and would, at times, threaten his very existence with all manner of self-inflicted pains through drink, drugs and sado-machoism.

In 1860 Swinburne published two verse dramas; The Queen Mother and Rosamond but it would not be until 1865 that Swinburne would achieve literary success with Atalanta in Calydon.

In 1861, Swinburne visited Menton on the French Riviera to recover from the effects of yet another period of excess use of alcohol, staying at the Villa Laurenti. From Menton, Swinburne then travelled on to Italy, where he journeyed widely.

After Elizabeth Rossetti's death from suicide in 1862, he and Rossetti moved to Tudor House at 16 Cheyne Walk in Chelsea. The stories that survive from his year with Rossetti are typical Swinburne. In one, Rossetti once had to tell him to keep down the noise — he and a boyfriend had been sliding naked down the bannisters and disturbing Rossetti's painting. He took a sardonic delight in what the critic and biographer, Cecil Lang, calls "Algernonic exaggeration": When people began to talk scathingly about his homosexuality and other sexual proclivities, he circulated a story that he had engaged in pederasty and bestiality with a monkey — and then eaten it. How many of the stories were true and how many invented is unclear. Oscar Wilde called him "a braggart in matters of vice, who had done everything he could to convince his fellow citizens of his homosexuality and bestiality without being in the slightest degree a homosexual or a bestialiser."

In December 1862, Swinburne accompanied Scott and his guests on a trip to Tynemouth. Scott writes in his memoirs that, as they walked by the sea, Swinburne declaimed the as yet unpublished 'Hymn to Proserpine' and 'Laus Veneris' in his lilting intonation, while the waves 'were running the whole length of the long level sands towards Cullercoats and sounding like far-off acclamations'.

Swinburne possessed a curious combination of frail health and strength. He was small and slightly built, but an excellent swimmer and the first to climb Culver Cliff on the Isle of Wight. He had an extremely excitable disposition: people who met him described him as a "demoniac boy" who would go skipping about the room declaiming poetry at the top of his voice. In this as in many things, moderation was not the standard for him. Excess was. Once or twice he had fits, thought to be epileptic, in public; but he made this condition much worse by drinking past excess to unconsciousness. More than once he was delivered to the door in the small of the night, dead drunk. Throughout the 1860s and '70s he rode an alcoholic cycle of dissolution, collapse, drying out at home in the country, then returning to London where he would begin the cycle all over again.

His mania for masochism, particularly flagellation, most probably started in early childhood at Eton and was encouraged by his later friendships with Richard Monckton Milnes (one of Tennyson's fellow Apostles), who introduced him to the works of the Marquis de Sade, and Richard Burton, the Victorian explorer and adventurer. Swinburne was an alcoholic and algolagniac (a desire for sexual gratification through inflicting pain on oneself or others; sadomasochism). He found life difficult, unfulfilling but still his poetic talents pushed to the fore.

Although Swinburne continued to publish some works in periodicals in 1865 he was granted recognition by both public and critics with Atalanta in Calydon written in the style of a classical Greek tragedy.

There followed "Laus Veneris" and Poems and Ballads (1866), with their sexually charged passages, absolutely decadent for polite Victorian society, which were attacked all the more violently as a result. The poems written in homage of Sappho of Lesbos such as "Anactoria" and "Sapphics" were especially savaged. The volume also contained poems such as "The Leper," "Laus Veneris," and "St Dorothy" which evoke both Swinburne's and a general Victorian fascination with the Middle Ages, and are explicitly mediaeval in style, tone and construction. With its publication came instant notoriety. He was now identified with indecent and decadent themes and the precept of art for art's sake.

Swinburne's meeting in 1867 with his long-time hero Mazzini, the Italian patriot living in England in exile, was the beginning of a poetical journey that now became more serious and more engaged with serious thought, initially leading to the political poems in the volume Songs Before Sunrise.

Also in 1867 he was introduced to Adah Isaacs Menken, the American actress, poet and circus rider, whose main fame seemed to be riding naked on a horse (in fact she wore tight nude coloured clothing) for her performance in the melodrama Mazeppa (itself based on a poem by Lord Byron). Although they had a short affair Adah's quote implies that Swinburne was not ready for a relationship that did not involve some self-sabotage; "I can't make him understand that biting's no use."

In 1879, with Swinburne nearly dead from alcoholism and dissolution, his legal advisor Theodore Watts-Dunton took him in, and was gradually successful in getting him to adapt to a healthier lifestyle. Swinburne lived the rest of his life at Watts-Dunton's house. He saw less and less of his old bohemian friends, who thought him a prisoner at The Pines, but his growing deafness also accounts for some of his decreased sociability. By now Swinburne was 42, and was moving from a young man of rebelliousness to a figure of social respectability. It was said of Watts-Dunton that he saved the man and killed the poet.

It is clear that Swinburne had an addictive personality, and clearly incapable of moderation in his pursuit of any chosen vices. This, of course, would both nourish and perhaps sabotage his poetic career. His poetry follows the somewhat clichéd pattern of early flourish and later decline; indeed some of the fresher pieces in the second and third series of Poems and Ballads (published in 1878 and 1889) were actually written during his days at Oxford. Nevertheless, his last collection, A Channel Passage, has some beautiful poems, including "The Lake of Gaube."

He is best remembered as the supreme technician in metre, with a versatility which exceeds even Tennyson's, but which lacks a corresponding emotional range. His obsessions are not widely enough shared; and if he cannot shock us by the strangeness of his desires nor the shrillness of his anti-theistical exclamations, often what remains is not enough to fully engage with the audience.

Swinburne is considered a poet of the decadent school, although he perhaps professed to more vice than he actually indulged in to advertise his deviance. Common gossip of the time reported that he also had a deep crush on the explorer Sir Richard Francis Burton, despite the fact that Swinburne himself abhorred travel. Fact and fiction are easily absorbed by the other so are difficult to untangle even now.

Many critics consider his mastery of vocabulary, rhyme and metre impressive, although he has also been criticised for his florid style and word choices that only fit the rhyme scheme rather than contributing to the meaning of the piece. A. E. Housman, although a critic, had great praise for his rhyming ability: to Swinburne the sonnet was child's play: the task of providing four rhymes was not hard enough, and he wrote long poems in which each stanza required eight or ten rhymes, and wrote them so that he never seemed to be saying anything for the rhyme's sake.

Throughout his career Swinburne published literary criticism of great worth. His deep knowledge of world literatures contributed to a critical style rich in quotation, allusion, and comparison. He is particularly noted for discerning studies of Elizabethan dramatists and of many English and French poets and novelists. As well he was a noted essayist and wrote two novels.

Swinburne was nominated for the Nobel Prize in Literature every year from 1903 to 1907 and then again in 1909.

H.P. Lovecraft, the master of the dark side and a decent poet himself, considered Swinburne "the only real poet in either England or America after the death of Mr. Edgar Allan Poe."

Swinburne was also responsible for devising a poetic form called the roundel, a variation of the French Rondeau form. In 1883 he published A Century of Roundels with several of the roundels dedicated to Dante's sister, the poet Christina Georgina Rossetti. Swinburne wrote to Edward Burne-Jones in 1883: "I have got a tiny new book of songs or songlets, in one form and all manner of metres ... just coming out, of which Miss Rossetti has accepted the dedication. I hope you and Georgie [his wife Georgiana] will find something to like among a hundred poems of nine lines each, twenty-four of which are about babies or small children".

Opinions of the Roundel poems move between those who find them captivating and brilliant, to others who find them merely clever and contrived. One of them, A Baby's Death, was set to music by the English composer Sir Edward Elgar as the song "Roundel: The little eyes that never knew Light".

After the first Poems and Ballads, Swinburne's later poetry was devoted more to philosophy and politics, including the unification of Italy, particularly in the volume Songs before Sunrise. He did not stop writing love poetry entirely, indeed it was only in 1882 that his great epic-length poem, Tristram of Lyonesse, was published, its contents lyrical rather than shocking. His versification, and especially his rhyming technique, remain of high quality to the end.

Algernon Charles Swinburne died of influenza, at the Pines in London on April 10th, 1909 at the age of 72. He was buried at St. Boniface Church, Bonchurch on the Isle of Wight.

Algernon Charles Swinburne – A Concise Bibliography

Verse Drama
The Queen Mother (1860)
Rosamond (1860)
Chastelard (1865)
Bothwell (1874)
Mary Stuart (1881)
Marino Faliero (1885)
Locrine (1887)
The Sisters (1892)
Rosamund, Queen of the Lombards (1899)

Poetry
Atalanta in Calydon (1865)*
Poems and Ballads (1866)
Songs Before Sunrise (1871)
Songs of Two Nations (1875)
Erechtheus (1876)*
Poems and Ballads, Second Series (1878)
Songs of the Springtides (1880)
Studies in Song (1880)
The Heptalogia, or the Seven against Sense. A Cap with Seven Bells (1880)
Tristram of Lyonesse (1882)
A Dark Month & Other Poems

A Century of Roundels (1883)
A Midsummer Holiday and Other Poems (1884)
Poems and Ballads, Third Series (1889)
Astrophel and Other Poems (1894)
The Tale of Balen (1896)
A Channel Passage and Other Poems (1904)

*Although formally tragedies, Atlanta in Calydon and Erechtheus are traditionally included with his poetry.

Criticism

William Blake: A Critical Essay (1868, new edition 1906)
Under the Microscope (1872)
George Chapman: A Critical Essay (1875)
Essays and Studies (1875)
A Note on Charlotte Brontë (1877)
A Study of Shakespeare (1880)
A Study of Victor Hugo (1886)
A Study of Ben Johnson (1889)
Studies in Prose and Poetry (1894)
The Age of Shakespeare (1908)
Shakespeare (1909)

Major Collections

The Poems of Algernon Charles Swinburne, 6 vols. 1904.
The Tragedies of Algernon Charles Swinburne, 5 vols. 1905.
The Complete Works of Algernon Charles Swinburne, 20 vols. Bonchurch Edition. 1925-7.
The Swinburne Letters, 6 vols. 1959-62.